Angels

Facts, Trivia &
Extraordinary Moments™

by BETTY O. BENNETT

Sweet Memories Publishing Company • Smyrna, TN 37167 • 1-615-459-4012

Art Direction & Typography by McClearen Design Studios
3901 Brush Hill Road, Nashville, TN 37216

Illustrated by Amanda Brooke Mangrum
Poems by Brandy Michelle Mangrum

Edited by Thomas L. Long

ISBN 0-9645218-5-7

PRINTED IN THE UNITED STATES OF AMERICA

PERSONAL DEDICATION

This book is dedicated to all the "angels" of the world and the people they were sent to watch over.

ACKNOWLEDGMENTS

Special thanks to my husband, Tom, who helps with my research; to my friends and family who shared their own special angel stories with me for this book; to my thirteen year old twin daughters, Brandy and Brooke for the beautiful poems and illustrations; to Julie, Brad, Dan and Mike, who had faith in me before I had faith in myself; and to William D. Webber, co-author of *A Rustle of Angels*, for his advice and words of encouragement. Without realizing it, he acted as my "guardian angel." Also a very special "thank you" to Betty Frost for her proofreading skills.

Thank you all so much!

INTRODUCTION

A few years ago you could not discuss the subject of angels in a group of people without being thought of as more than a little strange. The only time you might see an angel would be at Christmas, perhaps on the top of your tree.

Today, however, there is a proven fascination with angels. Most doll artists have their own angel dolls. Some even have a whole series of angel dolls. You can buy angel pins, earrings, necklaces and charms; angel figurines, plates, plaques, angel cards, stationery and candles; angel coffee mugs, and angel stamps. You can buy record albums and tapes with "music of the angels." Did I mention you can even buy books about angels?

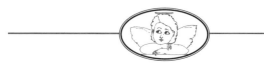

Angels have been discovered on the afternoon soaps. Last season on "Loving," Ava was accidentally shot. While in the hospital, she had a near-death experience, and was met by her dead uncle (looking very angel-like). He showed her a glimpse of her future and reluctantly sent her back to the living. Her family, of course, thought she had perhaps been unconscious a little too long.

Although this sudden interest in angels does make me a little more optimistic about the fate of mankind, I have to ask myself, why? The only conclusion I can come up with is that people are faced with so many problems today, we want or need to believe in something positive, perhaps a higher power watching over us.

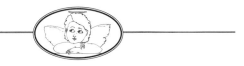

According to the Bible, everyone is assigned their own guardian angel at birth. I believe this is true even though mine seems to be "out to lunch" or "on vacation" at times. I do have to say that my guardian angel has been with me through the most critical times of my life, and for that I am thankful. I will relate some of those stories to you in this book.

I know you will find this book interesting and I hope it will touch your heart in some personal way.

Betty O. Bennett

Q. What is an angel?

A. Malcolm Goodwin answers that question eloquently in his book, *Angels, An Endangered Species:* "Angels are a landscape in which reality, myth, fantasy, legend, dreams and supernatural visions all appear hopelessly entangled."

Actually, angels are not endangered since they never die, nor do they increase or decrease in size. Although we like to picture chubby little baby angels, according to the Bible, they do not exist.

Q. Who is an angel?
A. One of the immortal beings attendant upon God.

Q. Where did the word "angel" come from?
A. The word angel is ancient Greek for "messenger."

This was a common job for angels in the Bible.

Angels are mentioned approximately 300 times in the Bible.

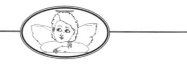

Angels belong to an order of supernatural spirit beings of which there seems to be many classes.

According to Hebrew beliefs, angels could have been created fifteen billion years ago. No one knows for sure.

Q. When did Christianity begin?
A. When an angel appeared to Mary in a dream telling her she was going to have a child and he should be named "Jesus," who is the Son of God.

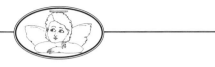

An angel also appeared in a dream to Mary's husband Joseph, telling him of the immaculate conception.

At the birth of Jesus in Bethlehem, a host of angels appeared to shepherds to say that the Son of God was born and they should follow the shining star to the baby Jesus.

In past history, religions, both primitive and sophisticated, have believed that spiritual beings have power from the "other world."

Not only are angels inseparable from God, they are indivisible from their witness.

Many theologians believe angels were created before the beginning of the world.

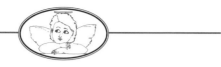

The Swedish mystic Swedenborg once said: "I am well aware that many will say that no one can possibly speak with spirits and angels so long as he is living in the body; many say it is all fantasy, others recount such things to win credence, while others will make other kinds of objections. But I am deterred by none of these: for I have seen, I have heard, I have felt."

Many other people are as sincere as Swedenborg in their belief that they have encountered a genuine angel with a genuine message.

Q. Do angels really exist?
A. The fact that most people have not seen an angel does not mean that they do not exist.

According to Thomas Aquinas, a top angel scholar of the Middle Ages, angels are 100% pure spirits, having no matter of mass and taking up no space -- like a thought.

Q. Do angels ever appear in the flesh?
A. Yes, occasionally. "Remember to welcome strangers in your home. There were some who did and welcomed angels without knowing it." (Hebrews 13:2)

Q. Where was the first depiction of an angel found?
A. Archaeologists uncovered an "angel" engraved in stone in the city of Ur in the Middle East. This city is over 4000 years old. This is thought to be the first depiction of an angel yet discovered.

Q. What is the Heavenly Hierarchy?
A. According to the Hebrews, the universe is a Cosmos Hierarchy with God at the center and the upper triad radiating from the center.

According to the text of the *Celestial Hierarchies* of Dionysius and the *Summa Theologica* by Thomas Aquinas, there are nine celestial orders orbiting the throne of God, similar to that of our own planetary system.

HIGHEST TRIAD

THE FIRST CHOIR: Seraphim

The Seraphs are normally accepted to be the highest order of God's angelic attendants. They are in direct union with God and as such are beings of pure light.

THE SECOND CHOIR: Cherubim

In both Judaic and Christian beliefs, God is said to have placed the Cherubim east of Eden and the ever turning sword to guard the way to the Tree of Life. A Cherubim is one of knowledge and wisdom.

THE THIRD CHOIR: Thrones

These angels are portrayed as the great "wheels" or the "many eyed ones." The Thrones are said to inhabit the third or the fourth heaven.

A Seraphim quavers at the highest angelic frequency. The Cherub, on the next rotating ring around the source, has a vibration rate which is a little lower. The Thrones of the third ring indicate the point at which matter begins to appear.

MIDDLE TRIAD

THE FOURTH CHOIR: Dominions

These angels are channels of compassion living within the second heaven. The ruling lords are said to be Zadkiel, Hashmal, Yabriel and Muriel.

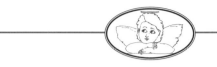

Hashmal is known as the "fire speaking angel."

THE FIFTH CHOIR: Virtues

These angels of grace give blessings from on high, usually in the form of miracles. They appeared in the Ascension of Christ where two provided His escort to heaven. Two Virtues gave assistance at the birth of Cain.

THE SIXTH CHOIR: Powers

Dynamis, Potentiates and Authorities were said to be the first angels created by God. As chief of the order, Cama-el vacillates between good and evil. His name means "he who sees God." His powers inhabit the perilous border region between the first and second heaven. He is commander of 144,000 angels of devastation, punishment, vengeance and death. Whether these powers serve God or the devil remains undetermined.

LOWEST TRIAD

The third triad of Principalities, Archangels and Angels are rooted within the first heaven. All three orders are most exposed and defenseless to any corrosion of the flesh. Angels from these orders are most well known, possibly because they are most like us.

THE SEVENTH CHOIR: Principalities

In the beginning, the Princedoms were seen as an order which was in charge of nations and great cities on Earth. The great prince of strength, Cervill, is said to have aided David in the slaying of Goliath.

THE EIGHTH CHOIR: Archangels

Of all the angelic orders, these have the largest claim to fame. Four names which appear regularly are: Michael, Gabriel, Raphael and Uriel.

Dionysius tells us that archangels are "messengers which carry divine decrees." They are believed to be the most important mediators between God and Heaven in their constant battle with the Sons of Darkness.

Following are a few of the most well-known archangels:

ARCHANGEL MICHAEL

His name means "who is as God." In most Christian beliefs he is the "greatest." He and Gabriel are the only two actually mentioned in the Old Testament, except for Raphael who was presented in the Catholic *Book of Tobit*.

Michael's notable deeds have captured the popular imagination far more than any other angel. He is said to have wiped out, single-handedly and overnight, 185,000 men from the army of the Assyrian king, Sennercherib, who was threatening Jerusalem in 701 B.C.

He stopped the hand of Abraham who was about to sacrifice his son, Isaac.

According to Jewish beliefs, it was Michael who came to Moses in the midst of a burning bush.

He is known as the undisputed hero in the first war against Satan. In single combat he defeated the arch-fiend and hurled him down from heaven.

It is foretold in Daniel that when the world is once again in real trouble, Michael will return. Many scholars believe this century will be the one in which he will reveal himself once more, in all his glory. It is said that Michael will come down from heaven with "the keys of the abyss and a great chain in his hand," and will bind the Satanic dragon for 1000 years. (Revelation 20:1)

ARCHANGEL GABRIEL

Gabriel is said to sit on the left hand side of God and is considered the Angel of Truth.

In Judeo-Christian lore, he is the Angel of the Resurrection, Annunciation, Mercy, Revelation and Death.

It was Gabriel who appeared to Daniel to tell him of the coming of a messiah, the same message he told to Mary 1000 years later in the Annunciation.

Before speaking to Mary, he had just announced to Zacharias the coming of John the Baptist.

ARCHANGEL RAPHAEL

Raphael is known as "the shining one who heals." He is also known to be the ruling prince of the second heaven.

He is chief of the order of Virtues, guardian of the Tree of Life in Eden and one of the seven Angels of the Throne. This he relates to Tobias in the *Book of Tobit*.

He is said to be both the chummiest and funniest of all the angelic flock, and is often depicted chatting merrily with some unsuspecting mortal.

He is also known as Angel of the Sun.

Raphael gave Noah a book which gave him the guidance he needed to build the ark.

He is declared to be "one of the four presences set over all the diseases and all the wounds of the children of men."

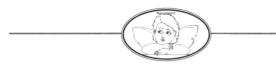

ARCHANGEL URIEL

It is said that Uriel is one of the four angels of the presence. Uriel, meaning "Fire of God," is identified in later scriptures with Phanuel, "Face of God."

He is often identified as the cherub who stands "at the gate of Eden with a fiery sword," or as the angel who "watches over thunder and terror."

He is said to be the first angel to change into a man.

He was the messenger sent to warn Noah that the world was going to end by a great flood.

According to the "Sibylline Oracles," Uriel will break the gates of Hades on the Day of Judgment.

ARCHANGEL RAGUEL

Raguel is known as one "who watches over the good behavior of the angels." He could possibly be one of the most overworked angels, as angels are very vulnerable when it comes to corruption.

It was Raguel who delivered Enoch to Heaven.

Among his other duties, he is believed to be an angel of earth and a guardian of the second heaven.

In 745 A.D., Raguel, along with Uriel, suffered the indignity of being excluded from the saintly calendar by a church council held by Pope Zachary.

The Revelation of John reads: "Then shall he send the angel Raguel saying; go sound the trumpet for the angels of cold and snow and ice and bring together every kind of wrath upon them that stand on the left."

ARCHANGEL REMIEL

In early records, he is known as Jeremiel, "Mercy of God."
This name identifies him as the "Lord of Souls awaiting
Resurrection."

He is the one "whom God sets up" in order to bring the
souls to Judgment.

He appears as one of the seven archangels who stand
before God.

ARCHANGEL RAZIEL

Raziel has the intriguing title of the "Angel of the Secret Regions and of the Supreme Mysteries."

He wrote the *Book of the Angel Raziel* "wherein all celestial and earthly knowledge is set down."

He presented the book to Adam, who passed it on to Enoch, who used much of it in the *Book of Enoch.* It was then given to Noah, then to Solomon.

ANGELOLOGY AND THE TREE OF LIFE

The Tree of Life had seven branches reaching to the heavens and seven roots in the earth. These were related to the seven mornings and seven nights of the week and correspond to the seven Archangels of the Christian hierarchy.

Man is situated in the middle of the tree suspended between heaven and earth. The enormous forces which flow around him create magnetic fields which are grouped in harmonious couples.

Brooke M.

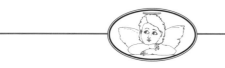

In numerous cultures throughout the world, there are legends of paradise gardens with a magical tree of everlasting life at its center. This tree has an angel to protect it from the unworthy. In the spiritual crucible of the Near and Middle East, this particular archetype has become the Tree guarded by the Cherub, the Jewish Sefiroth, the seven-branched candlestick and the Tree of the Freemasons.

Brooke M.

32

THE NINTH CHOIR: Angels

This is the last order of the celestial hierarchy and the one closest to humans. The Hebrew term for angel is mal'akh, meaning "a messenger." This brings us to the modern concept of angels being an intermediary between the Almighty and human mortals.

The greatest early source of names and angelic functions comes from the three Chronicles of the Hebrew patriarch, Enoch.

This Chronicle did not turn up in complete form until the 18th century when an original copy was found in the Ethiopic Church.

GUARDIAN ANGELS

It is believed that these angels appeared around eight thousand years before Christ. These ministering angels advised the seventy nations during Noah's time.

The earliest record tells of seventy administering angels led by Michael.

Michael, Raphael, Gabriel and Uriel are believed to be at the head of the guardian angels, one of the sub-classes of ministering angels. These angels are also in charge of nations, states and cities.

In early scriptures, Rabbis mentioned only four nations with their guardian angels by name. Many angels fell. Michael, in charge of Israel, remains unimpeachable.

The Egyptian guardian, Rahab, attempted to stop Moses and the Hebrews from escaping across the Red Sea.

Of all the protecting angels, only Michael managed to stay uncorrupted.

According to the "Talmud," from which the basis of orthodox Judaism is formed, every Jew is assigned several thousand angels at birth.

Christians have no official policy as far as guardian spirits are concerned, however, there are records which imply that two are entrusted to guide each Christian.

A Christian children's poem expands this number to four.

"Four angels to my bed,
four angels around my head,
One to watch and one
to pray, and
two to bear my soul away."

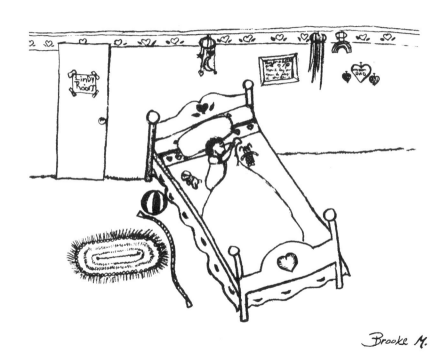

Brooke M.

Enoch mentions the mysterious Grigori or "Sons of God."

The term Grigori or Watcher can mean "those who watch," "those who are awake," or "the ones who never sleep."

The chief of one group of seven watchers, Santanael, first disobeyed the Lord and the group was punished.

They were held in a penal area within the fifth heaven which is described as reeking of sulfur.

Enoch was the grandfather of Noah and so could record, in detail, the great flood which was meant to destroy the world.

It is believed there were three distinct orders of angels in the lower level. At the top were seven Archangel rulers, who were known as the aristocratic two-eyed serpents.

Each ruled around 496,000 innumerable groups of ministering angels who were known as the one-eyed serpents.

Last came the working class watchers or guardian angels.

MUSICIAN ANGELS

Uriel is often said to be The Angel of Music. In Islam, we find this is Israfel. The Rabbis gave the title of the "Master of Heavenly Song" to Metatron or Shemiel.

Q. Are angels literate?
A. Yes, considering the messages they deliver are in the native language of the witness.

Q. What is believed to be the official angelic tongue?
A. Hebrew, Latin or Greek

THE THIRD WING

Heaven's above and Earth is below the seven celestial mansions. The number seven is one of the mystical marvels of our universe. Almost all religious and occult systems include the number seven somewhere close to their holiest of holy sanctums.

It is said that the tower of Babel was a tiered tower with the Almighty "seated on a great white throne surrounded by winged cherubim," in the highest of the seven heavens.

This concept predates the Hebrew hierarchy by one thousand five hundred years and the Christian version by over three thousand years.

Patriarch Enoch will lead us on a tour of the Seven Heavens, as he is an excellent guide.

FIRST HEAVEN

This is said to have been the home of Adam and Eve. It is the lowest Heaven and is at the edge of our own world.

Gabriel is the angel in charge of the first heaven.

This heaven contains clouds and winds, the Upper Waters and is the home of two hundred astronomer-angels who watch after the stars.

According to Enoch, "We landed in the first heaven and there they showed me a very great sea, much bigger than the inland sea where I lived." He describes it as being "A treasury of snow, ice, clouds and dew."

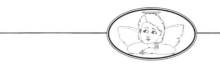

SECOND HEAVEN

Raphael is the angel ruler.

This is where the fallen angels are imprisoned.

Both Moses and Enoch visited this heaven which is said to be the home of John the Baptist.

St. Paul said, "The Angel brought me down from the third heaven and led me into the second heaven, and led me again to the firmament."

Sinners are chained there in complete darkness awaiting judgment.

THIRD HEAVEN

The angel ruler is Anahel.

A few authorities place Gehenna North of Eden, where volcanic fires burn continuously, polluting the air with sulfurous fumes, and a river of flames flow through a desolate land of cold and ice.

Here the wicked sinners are punished and tortured.

While to the south in the paradise lands, it is believed that divine bees store manna-honey for the delight of the virtuous.

There is a vast orchard with thousands of fruit trees, including the Tree of Life under which God takes a nap whenever he visits.

Two rivers flow from Eden: One flows with milk and honey, and the other with wine and oil.

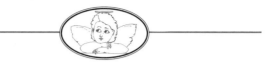

Two or three hundred Angels of Light guard the garden to which all the perfect souls come after death.

St. Paul was taken to the third heaven which had a gate with pillars of gold.

FOURTH HEAVEN

The ruling Prince is Michael.

There are twelve gold gates in the circuit of the city and four rivers encircle it.

An angel said, "These four rivers flow abundantly for those who are in the land of promise. These are their names: the river of honey is called Phison, the river of milk is called Euphrates, the river of oil is called Geon, and the river of wine, Tigris."

Enoch said, "In this heaven is the Tree of Understanding, the fruit of which they eat and, thereby, obtain great purpose."

"I commented on how beautiful and attractive the tree was and Raphael, the archangel who was with me said: This is the Tree of Understanding; your ancestral father and mother ate of it and it made them realize that they were naked; so they were expelled from the garden."

There was another tree which attracted Enoch the scribe. This time archangel Michael answered his curiosity: "As for this fragrant tree, no human is allowed to touch it until the great selection; at that time The Great Lord of Judgments will decide on the length of life to be granted."

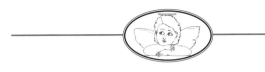

FIFTH HEAVEN

Archangel Metatron's twin brother, Sandelphon, is the ruling prince of this heaven.

Again, the north is set aside as a penal stockade.

Archangel Uriel said: "This is the prison of the angels and here they will be imprisoned for life."

The southern part of this heaven is very beautiful. It is said that hosts of ministering angels chant ceaselessly all through the night.

SIXTH HEAVEN

Domain of duality, Zebul rules by night and Sabath rules by day.

Seven Phoenixes and seven Cherubim dwell here. They chant and sing in praise of God, and a great host of Shining Ones study astronomy.

There are other angels who study time, ecology, the seasons and humankind in a vast Building of Knowledge.

Enoch seems to be describing a vast Angelic University when he says: "And there I saw seven groups of Angels, very bright and wonderful, with their faces shining brighter than the sun."

"They were brilliant and all dressed alike and looked alike."

Some of the angels study the movement of the stars, the sun and the moon and record the peaceful order of the world.

These are some of the archangels who are promoted over the other angels.

SEVENTH HEAVEN

Cassiel is the ruling prince of this heaven.

This is the home of God on His Holy Throne, encompassed by Seraphim, Cherubim and Wheels all bathed in brilliant light.

Enoch describes this holiest of holies in rather surprising terms. "Two angels conducted me to a place where everybody was as bright as fire, but if they wished, could appear as ordinary men."

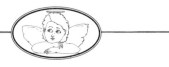

Enoch continues, "They brought me to a mountain whose summit reached to the heavens. There I saw lighted places and heard thunderous noises; and in the deepest part, there were lights which looked like a fiery bow and arrows with their quiver, and moving lights like a fiery sword."

There is no absolute proof that a Heavenly Hierarchy exists, however, it seems probable that there are intelligent forms of life in other galaxies and that some higher power created everything from the beginning.

There will be a time for all of us to see if there are angels and an Almighty Power to guide us to another world.

THE FEATHER, IN MEMORY OF YOU

*I once saw a feather, floating from the sky
but when I looked up, no bird was to be found.*

*So I glanced at the feather beside my shoe,
and picked it gently up from the ground.*

*After looking at the feather for quite some time,
I sensed a sudden warmth and glow.*

*While the thrills of the Heavens ran through my
mind I realized this was no ordinary feather at all.*

*Then I felt a tiny sprinkle upon my cheek,
like a cool shower on an Autumn's day.*

*And I won't forget the angel that was so unique
for its tears and the feather I have saved.*

By Brandy Mangrum

In the fourteenth century, half of Europe was destroyed by the Black Plague.

Both saints and angels were supposed to be able to stop such horrors, but neither did.

This caused a widespread distrust of all the church's excessive religious teachings.

The new Humanist ideas which challenged the angelic hierarchies also looked at Christ in a new way.

With new realities of astronomy, the whole concept of the seven heavens and the seven earths began to appear absurd.

The old belief that it was the spirits and holy angels who kept the universe turning was replaced by a new belief in "natural forces" like gravity.

During this era, the spiritual interests were being replaced by an excitement with the New World and scientific discoveries.

The immediate effect of the scientific approach was a procurement of new knowledge, which further eroded an already shaky house of angelic cards.

The Church's integrity concerning angels was challenged with the inception of scientific methodology.

People no longer believed they were guided by angelic forces.

New frontiers were opening in America and the old world of religion and angels no longer seemed interesting.

This foundational idea of the Church was successfully challenged by the newly arising Humanism by the middle of the 15th century. In retrospect, it seems that quite the reverse actually happened. Angels came to Earth.

THE NORTHERN STAR

An angel is like a Northern star,
to guide you places near and far.

Through loss of hope, or troubled heart,
through pain and suffering,
or when loved ones part.

There's a Northern star deep in your heart.

By Brandy Mangrum

Brooke M. 66

Q. What is Angelology?
A. Angelology is the study of angels.

Around 500 years after Christ, Pseudo-Dionysius, a mysterious Middle-Eastern writer, studied the angel names mentioned in the Bible.

From what he learned he wrote his version of the heavenly hierarchy.

Since he signed his name "Dionysius," ancient Christians mistook him for a famous early Christian by the same name.

As a result, his theory of angel organization was universally accepted in the Middle Ages.

Later it was proven that his manuscripts were written centuries after the real Dionysius lived.

His influence in the Middle Ages was still tremendous and his version of the hierarchy of angels is still the most well-known.

Q. Who is known as the "angelic doctor"?
A. Thomas Aquinas.

In A.D. 1215, Aquinas attempted to tell everything that was known about angels.

He gave fifteen lectures in one week. These lectures were written down and became his great work, the *Summa Theologica.*

The *Summa Theologica* is known as the most brilliant work ever written on the subject of angels.

Aquinas gathered information from the scripture and from tradition. Since scriptures do not answer many questions about angels, he added his own summations.

If you read the *Summa Theologica* today, you would see that many of his answers were based on the culture and traditions of his time.

Q. What is the Kabbalah?
A. Mystical writings so secret that they were handed down orally, from one master to another.

It was studied by the Jews in Germany, France, Spain and England during the time they were forced into religious isolation.

For this reason, the Kabbalah was never studied by the great medieval Christians.

The Kabbalah is so sacred and so complicated that it is
very difficult to understand.

According to the Kabbalah, the angel Metatron began his
journey as Enoch, a prophet in the Book of Genesis. He
led such a holy life that God took him to heaven, into the
first ranks of angels and named him Metatron, meaning
"closest to the throne."

In some centuries, angelology was studied more than in other centuries. During the 12th and 15th centuries, angelology was popular. By the late Renaissance, the interest in angelology was on the decline.

Around this time, however, Emanuel Swedenborg still saw angels and recorded what he saw.

He was a great theology professor in Sweden and lived from 1688 to 1772.

He wrote many books about his communications with angels.

Swedenborg stated that a spirit, or angel, not being composed of material substances, cannot reflect the sun's rays to be visible.

According to him, the only way an angel can be seen is when the angel assumes a material body, or when our spiritual eyes have been opened.

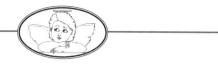

He states that angels breathe an atmosphere adapted to their angelic lungs, and that they can speak and write.

According to Swedenborg, angels have no power of their own. Their power comes from God.

If an angel doubts where his power came from, he instantly becomes weak.

Swedenborg's books teeter on the edge of bizarre and are not widely read today.

Brooke M. 76

Some people thought Swedenborg was insane, however, after he died, his followers in England founded a church based on his teachings.

Its members numbered over 100,000 worldwide.

Another philosopher influenced by Swendenborg was Rudolf Steiner. Steiner was born in 1861 in Czechoslovakia.

From the age of eight, he could see other worlds and creatures that normal people could not see.

He did not tell anyone about the conversations with these beings until he was forty years old.

From then until his death at the age of sixty-five, he taught and wrote about what he had seen and what he understood.

He was very brilliant, but many people thought he was crazy.

He investigated the world of physical substance to develop a model of a spiritual world.

Steiner identified his own hierarchy of angels which was different from that of Dionysius and Aquinas.

His version of the hierarchy was taken from Classical Greek as well as Judaic sources.

Steiner's "angels" were tied to earlier cosmic worlds.

He is said to have consorted with nature spirits and was surrounded by angels.

Steiner's theories, however, are very different from messages we get from saints.

In the 1600s, the blind Puritan poet, John Milton, wrote the twelve volume "Paradise Lost."

This work proved to be the greatest adventure poem in the English language.

It expands the story of the fall of Satan and of Adam and Eve in the Garden of Eden.

When Milton died in 1674, he had won a place in English literature next to Shakespeare.

Q. Do you have a guardian angel?

A. According to the Bible, everyone is assigned a guardian angel at birth.

Some say that many instances of "angelic help" actually come from deceased loved ones.

Any person or thing may be employed by God to do His will. This person or thing would become God's angel or messenger.

Others say the help could actually come from your subconscious mind.

Q. Can angels act as guides?
A. There have been many instances reported of angels leading lost people to safety.

Q. Do angels keep a record of our deeds?
A. It is said that our own minds record all of our actions.

Near-death survivors tell of having their whole lives flash
in front of them.

People who are hypnotized can remember details of their
past which they could not otherwise remember.

Q. What is an angel's halo?
A. Although we think of a halo as a golden disk around
   the head, it could actually be a symbol of its spirit
   body of light.

The German expression for "halo" is holy shine.

Q. How do angels think?

A. In John Ronner's book, *Do You Have A Guardian Angel?,* he writes, "For one thing, angels need fewer mental concepts to understand the world than we do, just as a genius draws more conclusions from the same facts than a dullard."

He goes on to say, "The higher the angel, the fewer concepts he needs to understand the universe because those fewer ideas are more far-reaching."

Q. Do angels know everything?
A. "No! Angels have superhuman knowledge.
They know more than people, but only God is
omniscient," as written in *A Rustle of Angels* by
William D. and Marilyn Carlson Webber.

For example, angels do not know when the Second
Coming of Christ will be. "But of that day and hour
knoweth no man, no, not the angels of heaven, but my
Father only." (Matthew 24:36)

Q. Do angels have bodies?
A. Some believe they only have spirit bodies, while others believe angels can take on bodies of their own when dealing with mortals.

Q. Is there an "Angel of Death"?
A. There have been many instances reported of dying patients speaking to someone that cannot be seen. Many times they address that person as though they know him. Sometimes it would be the name of their deceased husband, wife or parent.

According to psychic researcher, Walter Prince, besides dead friends and relatives standing in as "angels of death," plenty of evidence points to angels themselves acting as escorts to the beyond.

It has also been said that angel-like "beings of light" are often seen and are apparently telling the near-death victims that it is not their time to go. They are still needed here on earth.

Many of these near-death patients do not really want to come back to the living. When they do, however, they no longer fear death.

Many people have reported seeing their future during a near-death experience. After the experience, they could not remember the details of what they had seen, only that they had seen something.

These experiences seem to be timeless; they could be a brief moment, or centuries.

People who allegedly "left" their physical bodies during brushes with death have reported that they could think much more clearly in their "spirit bodies."

Persons who have encountered superhuman "beings of light" during near-death experiences report being lost in an overpowering love.

According to some of these near-death survivors, these "beings of light" would stress the importance of loving others on earth and of developing knowledge and wisdom.

Brooke M.

OH GLORIOUS DAY!

The Heaven's light shines in the sky,
for only God knows the reason why.

Until that day, Oh Glorious Day,
music playing from on high.

What it was I could not define
but it sent trickles down my spine.

Then a sweet aroma filled the air
of Jesus' feast and wine.

And then with pride the reason why,
was resting in my head.

Then glittered the path to the golden gate,
on which the angels led.

At once I knew my time had come,
not a nightmare I could see.

Yet on that day, Oh Glorious Day,
my soul would be set free.

By Brandy Mangrum

Q. Why do near-death patients see angels in so
many different forms?

A. Most likely they are all seeing the same form
but they would interpret it according to their own
personal religion.

Some suggest that the supernatural "beings of light" that
near-death patients see may merely be their own "highest
and best selves."

This may explain some of the guardian angel events but
there are still many left unexplained!

Q. Are angels real?
A. It would be doubtful that human beings would be the last step upward on the staircase before reaching God.

There are times when angels appear in a life-or-death situation, but sometimes they come quietly, leaving us to wonder why.

They could come at an important time, or at what we would consider to be an insignificant time.

Angels are not always sent to save a life, sometimes they intervene by giving us strength for a particular challenge or ordeal.

Angels often comfort people after the death of a loved one.

Q. Do angels sing and play harps?
A. Although we are not sure about the playing of harps, near-death survivors have reported hearing beautiful heavenly music.

Q. What do angels look like?

A. Usually angels are unseen, but sometimes they take on human form in order to do their work without scaring us.

The Bible does not explain how spirit beings can assume bodies, it simply states that sometimes we do not recognize them as angels because they look like us.

Some report seeing angels as beautiful beings with wings.

Others report them as a presence of light.

In Exodus 3:2, an angel appeared to Moses as flames in the burning bush.

In Psalm 104:4, angels are a flaming fire.

Some say they have seen an angel begin as a faint glow, and then change and light up the room.

Many observers tell of a pure white light; others describe different colors.

A dozen people could look at the same piece of art and all see something different in it.

Angels can show up at the most unexpected times.

When facing temptation, an angel is always just a prayer away.

Q. Why can't everyone see angels?
A. Physical eyes are not built to see the spirit world. Also, if you do not expect to see something, most likely you won't.

Q. How do angels communicate with us?

A. Have you ever gone to sleep after pondering a question concerning something very important to your future, only to awake the next morning with the answer? Perhaps your guardian angel spoke to you in your dreams.

Have you ever had a strong "hunch" or a "gut feeling" about something. This too could be the voice of your guardian angel.

They may communicate in other ways, but before you can hear, you must listen.

Q. Where might we meet an angel?
A. Most likely in an isolated area and when you are alone.

People see an angel only when an angel decides to be seen, or when it is God's will for the angel to be seen.

It would be unlikely to meet an angel at the mall or grocery store!

Sometimes angels come in the form of friends, but we seem to recognize them more when they appear as strangers.

Many explorers have reported a feeling of someone else being with them while in desolate regions of the country. Others felt a strange, unseen presence.

The feeling was so strong for some of them, they attempted to share their food with the presence.

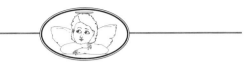

Q. When people die, do they become angels?
A. Although many may find this a comforting thought, according to the Bible, angels are not humans who have died.

People are born. Angels are created. Every angel has been created directly by God, from nothing.

Q. If all of this is true, what happens to infants when they die?

A. The angels carry them to heaven where they are placed in the arms of God.

Q. What are fallen angels?

A. They are angels who were thrown out of heaven for rebelling against God. These angels were led by Lucifer.

Lucifer, son of the morning, was the most outstanding angel God created, however, of his own choice, he sinned against God.

Because of his pride and desire to be like God himself, he influenced other angels to follow in his path of sin.

Bible scholars believe as many as one third of the angels fell with Lucifer.

God expelled them from heaven and Lucifer became known as Satan.

"There was war in heaven. Michael and his angels fought against the dragon, and the dragon and his angels fought back...The great dragon was hurled down---that ancient serpent called the devil, or Satan, who leads the whole world astray. He was hurled to the earth, and his angels with him." (Rev. 12:7-9)

Satan's primary function today is to tempt humans. (I might add he does a good job of that!)

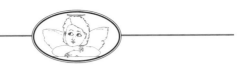

People find it easy to believe "the Devil made me do it."
Why can't they believe good angels can help them resist
these temptations.

Q. Why are demons sometimes confused with the Angel
of Death?

A. At one time Satan himself was known as the Angel of
Death, since death was considered evil. Now death
and evil are no longer connected, and the Angels of
Death we hear of today, are sent by God.

Demons, on the other hand, can cause depression and make us feel an emptiness so terrible that we plunge into drugs, sex or even murder in order to deaden the pain.

Q. With good angels and evil angels lurking around, how am I to know which is which?

A. Although the evil angels will try to disguise themselves, the following statements, known as the gift of discernment, should help.

1. The messages from the good angels will always agree
    with the Bible scriptures.

2. A message from God's angels will always be in the
    spirit of Christ.

3. A genuine encounter with a good angel will always
    glorify God, not the angel.

4. Good angels normally leave a person with a sense of
    peace and a greater love of God.

5. God's angels do not act to grant one person's selfish desire if it would hurt others.

6. Prayer should be used to confirm the genuineness of an encounter with an angel.

Q. Have angels always been here?
A. Only God always existed. The general theory is that angels came after God, then the universe, then man.

Q. Why do angels seem to help some people but ignore others?

A. Often it is meant for us to learn a lesson from problems or adversity.

For some people, trouble can be brought on by negative thinking like hate or worry. A person's negative thoughts can turn into reality.

By contrast, the positive thinker often attracts fortune and repels harm.

Q. What is a miracle?
A. Some say a miracle is a wonder that defies natural laws, while others say they may actually be the work of higher, still undiscovered laws.

Q. How do angels move around?
A. Just as your mind can travel from one thought to another, angels can move from the past, to the present, or to the future.

Brooke M.

Q. Since angels are spirits and can travel instantaneously, why are they depicted as having wings?

A. The early books of the Old Testament make no mention of wings. Possibly angels are pictured with wings as a symbol of rapid flight.

Q. How many angels are there?

A. So many you cannot count them all.

Q. Are angels male, female, both or neither?
A. In Jewish tradition, angels are masculine; in the Christian tradition they are androgynous, which means having both male and female characteristics, although after the Renaissance they are pictured with a more feminine appearance.

Q. Are angels immortal?
A. Angels are immortal. They never die.

Angels are much stronger than we are, however, their power is not physical, but spiritual.

One angel killed 185,000 Assyrians, enemies of Israel, in one night. (2 Kings 19:35)

One angel rolled away the stone from the door of the burial vault to let the women see that Jesus was not there. (Matthew 28:2)

A mighty angel lays hold of the dragon, binds him with a great chain and casts Satan into the bottomless pit. (Revelation 20)

It was one angel that opened the prison doors at night to deliver the apostles. (Acts 5:19)

Q. What are the chief functions of angels?
A. To carry out commands of God for His children here on earth.

Angels can appear as thoughts, voices, dreams, signs, visions or they can appear as people.

In *A Book of Angels*, Sophy Burnham writes, "Angels come in all sizes, shapes and colors, visible and invisible to our eyes. But you are always changed after having seen one."

It amazes me that so much time has been spent by medieval theologians and by more modern day philosophers, trying to figure out the rank of angels and where they live.

Angels merely live in heaven,
the space of eternity,
and hopefully, in our hearts!

THE ANGEL

The angel comes, the angel goes,
the angel flows - - where nobody knows.

Is it in the sky, flying oh so high,
or on the ground, not making a sound?

Wherever the angel goes or stays,
it's there to guide you through your days.

Whenever you're scared, the angel is bolder,
and tells you what's right, while on your shoulder.

Like a guiding map, or a guarding knight,
the angel is there, to win the fight.

By Brandy Mangrum

Brooke M.

Close Encounters

Of An

Angelic Kind

The first three stories relate events I experienced personally. Next, I included a letter from my aunt telling about some angelic happenings in her life.

The other stories were told to me by family or friends. I would like to thank them for sharing with us.

THE CASE OF THE FLYING HOOD

A few summers ago my husband and I decided to drive to Texas to visit his son. Since my brother was living in Louisiana at the time, we planned to stop and see him on our way. One night while just outside New Orleans we decided to go into town for dinner.

We got on the interstate and headed for New Orleans. Traffic was moving much too fast since we were about to cross a very long bridge. Everyone must have been going 75 or 80 miles per hour. As we were crossing the bridge, the hood on the car right in front of us broke

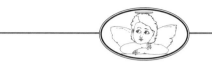

off and came flying towards us. It happened so fast I doubt we could have swerved even if there were a place we could swerve to.

For a split second, we thought we were all going to die when suddenly the wind caught the flying hood and lifted it right over our car. Immediately we heard tires squealing behind us.

Since everyone was moving so fast, I don't know if the hood hit someone behind us, or if it just hit the road. All I know is that we were spared. Our Guardian Angel was watching after us.

TWINS???

At thirty-something, I desperately wanted another child. My only child was a daughter and she was eleven. After only four months, I thought I was pregnant. I bought a home pregnancy kit and crossed my fingers. Bright and early the next morning, after carefully reading all the instructions, I used the kit. Well, like they say on T.V., I was "in the pink."

Only a few days had passed and I was already picking out names. Suddenly I started having severe pains in my lower back. I called my doctor and he told me to stay in bed the rest of the weekend and come to his office on Monday.

By Monday, the pain was so bad I could barely stand up. As soon as the doctor examined me he made arrangements for me to go to the hospital. I was having a miscarriage and he wanted to perform a D and C as soon as possible.

My first thought was what did I do wrong to cause this. The doctor assured me that this was nature's way of taking care of mistakes. It was little consolation at the time. I was very upset about losing this baby, and I was equally concerned that due to my age, this could be my last chance.

After the D and C, my doctor advised me to wait at least six months before trying again. I followed his advice

and one year later I was expecting again. I started prenatal care immediately. I was considered to be high risk due to my age and the fact that I had already lost one baby.

They monitored me very closely and everything was going along fine until my seventh month. The doctor measured my stomach, looked at my chart and measured it again. He asked me if I could possibly be wrong about my dates and I said no. Then he asked if diabetes ran in my family and I told him it did. Next he asked me if twins ran in my family, and I answered yes.

He immediately scheduled me for a glucose tolerance test. It was normal. Next he scheduled me for an

ultrasound. I will never forget that day if I live to be one hundred.

The technician performed the test and told me my doctor would have to give me the results. I informed them that I was not leaving until I knew how many babies I was carrying. On that happy note the technician began looking for a doctor.

Four weeks later, my husband and I were the proud parents of identical baby girls. We felt doubly blessed. I have always felt God sent me two children to make up for the one I lost.

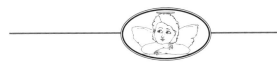

PLEASE SAVE MY CHILD

It was January of 1981. Brandy and Brooke were eighteen months old and had been on antibiotics for what seemed like all winter. Since they were premature and still very small for their age, they were very susceptible to everything going around. I worked, so they went to day care.

This particular day started off like any other day. I dropped the girls off at day care and began my 25 mile drive to work. Around 3:00, I received a call from the day care center. The director said Brandy was fine during

lunch but when she awoke from her nap, she seemed to have a high fever.

I left work immediately and drove the 25 miles to the day care center as fast as I could. When I arrived, I saw Brandy sitting on the floor, propped up against the wall. When I picked her up, she felt like a rag doll. She was burning up with fever and other than her eyes being opened, she was totally lifeless. I put her in the car, drove home and called her doctor. He told me to take her to Vanderbilt Hospital right away.

My thirteen year old daughter, Tina, was home from school by now and my husband was home from work.

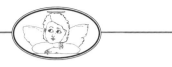

Brooke stayed home with her dad, and Tina and I headed
for Vanderbilt with Brandy. I was so scared that the drive,
which normally takes forty-five minutes, only took me
twenty. Finally, we arrived at the emergency room. They
rushed us right in. Apparently my doctor had already
alerted them.

After examining her, the doctors suspected spinal
meningitis. They needed my permission to do a spinal tap.
I had heard of this disease but was not aware how serious it
was. There are two types, viral and baterial. She had
bacterial, which was at least treatable. I asked if she
would be okay but the doctors gave me no assurance that

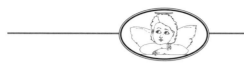

she would even live. They added that if she lived, she would most likely suffer brain damage.

Brandy was on an IV for thirteen days. Finally I began to see an improvement in her. In a few more days, she was discharged.

Brandy is almost fourteen now. As you can see by her poems, she does not have brain damage, but is a perfectly normal (I use this term loosely) teenager. I know her guardian angel was with her.

A LETTER FROM AUNT ETTA

Betty, I'm afraid my angel stories won't be of much help to you. I sometimes have a problem distinguishing between angel help and the help of the Holy Spirit, but I believe the angels' ministry largely has to do with our physical health and well being. I believe this help begins at infancy and continues throughout life. They are always watching us.

With that in mind, think of all the little children we have seen and known whose parents do not watch after them very well, yet they are safe from many things that

could harm them. I believe they are protected by angels.

I know a little girl named Sara who is three years old. Sara had learned how to unlock the front door of their home and did so at 3:00 in the morning while her mother was asleep. The police found her wandering around in the street. She could have just as easily been kidnapped, raped or hit by a car. Angels were watching over her even though her mother was not.

Another example of angel help came back in 1987. My sister Ellen lay in the hospital for two weeks, eyes closed, no speech or movements. I don't know if she was in a coma or not. On June 6, 1987, I visited her in the

hospital. No one else was there at the time. I leaned over, kissed her and whispered in her ear, "Ellen, just let go."

In about one hour, I received a call from my nephew Chuck Dailey. He was at the hospital. He said Ellen had just died. I truly believe an angel came down and escorted her to Heaven.

On another occasion, my daughter and I were on our way home from church Just outside of town, the road got real slippery from the snow and ice. The car started sliding sideways and landed straddled over a very deep ditch. We just knew it was going to flip over, but it just stopped.

Later a tow truck was able to get us back on the road without a scratch on the car, or us. Angels were definitely watching over us.

I'm sure you've heard the song "All day and all night, angels watching over me." Well, I believe it with all my heart. I've never thought a lot about angels until recent years. I always thought I would be afraid to live alone. After my husband died nine years ago, I read in the Bible, "He will establish the border of the widow." I believe the angels are encamped around my house, and I am not afraid.

Etta Kaufman - Ohio

THE CASE OF THE MIXED-UP BLOOD WORK

Suffice to say that I do not go to doctors unless I absolutely have to. Two years ago I went to my doctor for a routine physical. Everything seemed to be normal. I was overweight, had high blood pressure and was told that my body was a physical wreck. As I said, everything was normal. They drew blood for the usual tests and I left the office with around two hundred dollars less than I went in with. It was Friday and I was looking forward to a restful weekend.

The next day my phone rang and my wife answered. I didn't know who it was at the time, but I could tell something was wrong. When she hung up, she told me it was my doctor. It seems that my blood count was only half what it should be, indicating that I must be bleeding internally. Of course our first thought was cancer. The doctor wanted to put me in the hospital to run more tests. I called him back myself and told him I felt too good to be that sick and I refused to go into the hospital for tests. He said in that case at least come back in on Monday for another blood test.

This was probably the longest weekend of my life. Even though I was sixty-three at the time, I felt I had just begun to live and I was sure not ready to die. I considered myself Catholic and although I didn't attend church regularly, I did believe in God. That night I prayed harder than I had ever prayed in my life. I made a promise to God that if he would make my blood test come back normal, I would go to church every Sunday. Early Monday morning, I went back to the doctor for my second blood test. Again, I had to wait twenty-four hours for the results. The next day finally arrived and I received a call

from my doctor. He said this second test was normal. He couldn't understand it, but I could. He ordered a third test. It also came out normal!

You could say the lab technition made an error on my first blood test, or just maybe God granted me a second chance at life.

Tom - Nashville

LISA'S STORY

After dinner one evening, my husband, our two daughters, and I were taking a walk in our neighborhood. As we turned onto our street, a car came speeding around the corner. I took off after Jessica, but realized I could not make it in time. At that instant, I saw a hand reach down, pick Jessica up, and move her out of the way just as the car reached her. I believe to this day, that it was the hand of her guardian angel and I am very thankful to have her with me.

JEANNINE'S EXPERIENCE

Three years ago I was driving home from a job interview that I knew I didn't get. I was very upset and crying because I had no job, but I had many bills to pay. In addition to this, I was very uncertain about a relationship I was in. I was driving down the interstate, listening to gospel music, and crying like a baby with no idea of how to handle this situation. About that time, I felt God's hand go around me and heard him say, "It's okay, I've got you and you're going to be fine." From that moment on I knew everything would work out for the best, and it did.

DADDY'S PASSAGE

My dad had been sick with Alzheimer's disease for almost seven years and in his last six months had reached a permanently vegetated state. He couldn't move unless we moved him, he couldn't speak, he couldn't eat, he couldn't even focus his eyes. He could recognize no one.

On the night my dad died, my sister, my best friend and I had been keeping vigil for the entire day. As we stood by Daddy's bed, all of a sudden the atmosphere within the room changed. It felt similar to static electricity. My sister also noticed the change within the

room. She said, "Look at the hair on my arms. It's stand-ing straight up!" My friend and I looked at our arms and indeed the same phenomenon was occurring. Within a few seconds after feeling this odd change in the atmosphere, my sister said, "Look, look at Daddy!" As I stood on one side of Daddy's bed and my sister stood on the other, we watched as Daddy slowly turned his head toward my sister. He looked at her, smiled and then turned his head towards me and smiled. Daddy then turned his head forward, took two or three breaths, and died.

As my sister and I stood there weeping, my friend

said, "Look, the electricity in the air is gone." I looked at my arms and it was true, the hair once again laid down and the static was gone.

I have since talked about these events with several different people and have thus drawn the following conclusions. I now believe with all my heart that the minute we felt the electricity in Daddy's room was the very minute angels were sent from heaven and entered that room. I believe that God in his mercy and kindness allowed Daddy to recognize my sister and I in his last seconds on earth. I also truly believe that those angels that

exuded that electricity in Daddy's room came specifically to take my Dad, wrap him in their majestic wings, and usher him into the very presence of God.

One night several months after my Dad died, following an extremely stressful day, I collapsed into bed, totally exhausted, both mentally and physically. I remember saying to my husband before I closed by eyes in sleep, "I wish that Daddy were here to take care of me."

Several hours later, I was awakened from what I first thought to be simply a dream. In my dream I could see Daddy on the ceiling of my bedroom hovering over me. He was dressed in a long flowing white robe, and had a

glow about his head like none I had ever seen. As he hovered above my bed, Daddy repeated over and over, "Don't worry Sam (this was Daddy's favorite nickname for me). Everything is going to be okay. Things will work out. I'm watching over you."

When I awakened, I continued to see this vision of Daddy above the bed. It was so real that I awakened my husband and asked him repeatedly if he could see Daddy above the bed. My husband never saw what I had seen and after a few minutes the vision disappeared.

I truly believe that this was more than just a dream.

I believe that my Dad is in Heaven and perhaps has taken on some angelic qualities. I believe his visit that night was to encourage, uplift, and strengthen me during a very difficult time in my life.

Terrie Johnson
Lenexa, Kansas

I know many of you have had close angelic encounters of your own. I hope they were pleasant experiences.

If you would like to share your stories, you may write to me at:

> P.O. Box 414
> Smyrna, TN 37167

> Betty O. Bennett

BIBLIOGRAPHY

"Do You Have A Guardian Angel?"
John Ronner   Mamre Press
Oxford, Al.

"A Rustle of Angels"
William D. Webber & Marilynn Carson Webber
Zondervan Publishing House
Grand Rapids, Mi.

"Angels: An Endangered Species"
     Malcolm Godwin   Simon & Schuster
                             New York, N.Y.

"A Book Of Angels"
     Sophy Burnham   Ballantine Books

"The Angels of God"
     M.R. DeHaan, M.D.
                       Radio Bible Class Publication

....other items available from Sweet Memories Publishing

BOOKS

> Collectible Dolls; Facts & Trivia, Volume One
> Teddy Bears: Facts, Trivia & Interesting Stories

CASSETTES/CD's - Lullabies for infants and babies

> A Child's Gift of Lullabyes - GRAMMY Finalist!
> Rock-A-Bye Volume 1 - GRAMMY Winner!
> Rock-A-Bye Volume 2 - GRAMMY Finalist!
> Snuggle Up - GRAMMY Finalist!
> Little Sleepy Eyes - GRAMMY Finalist!
> A Child's Gift of Bedtime Stories

To order, call 1-800-925-1290 (Anytime)
We accept Mastercard or Visa